The Present

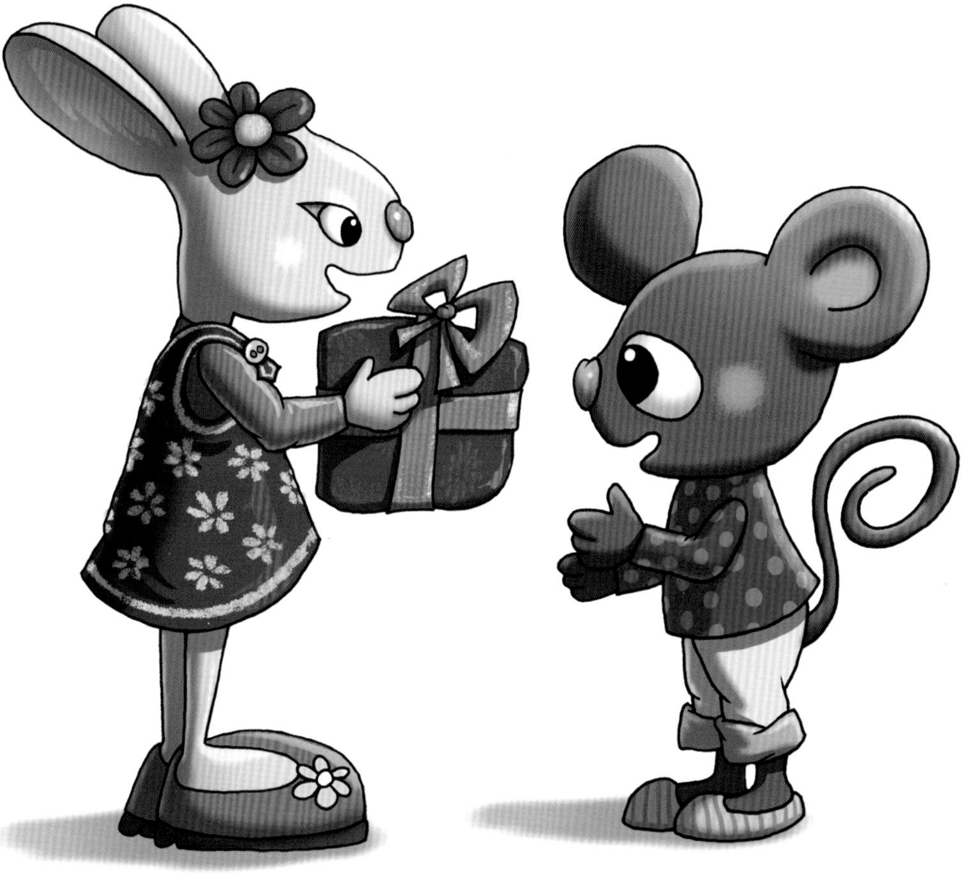

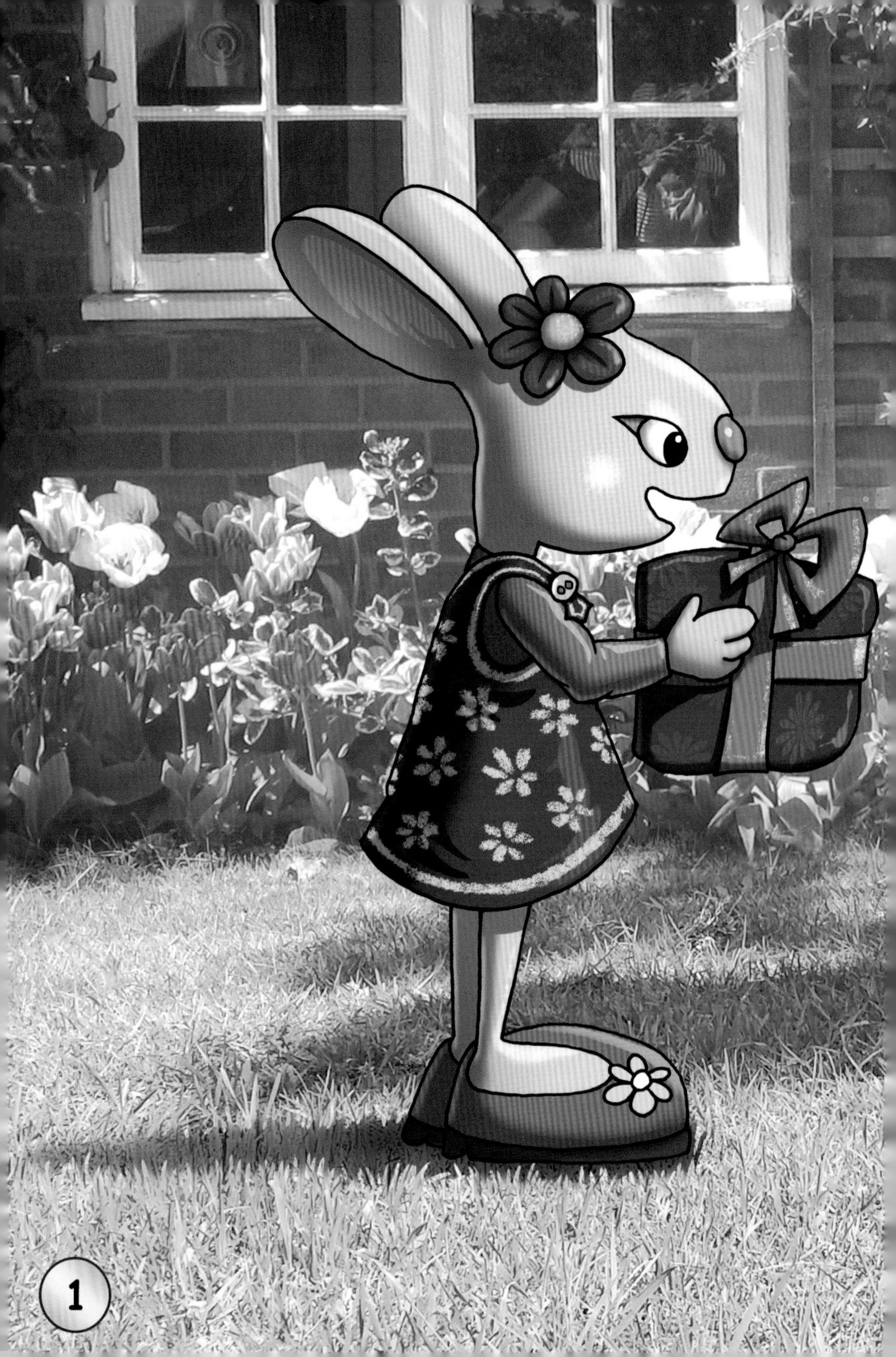

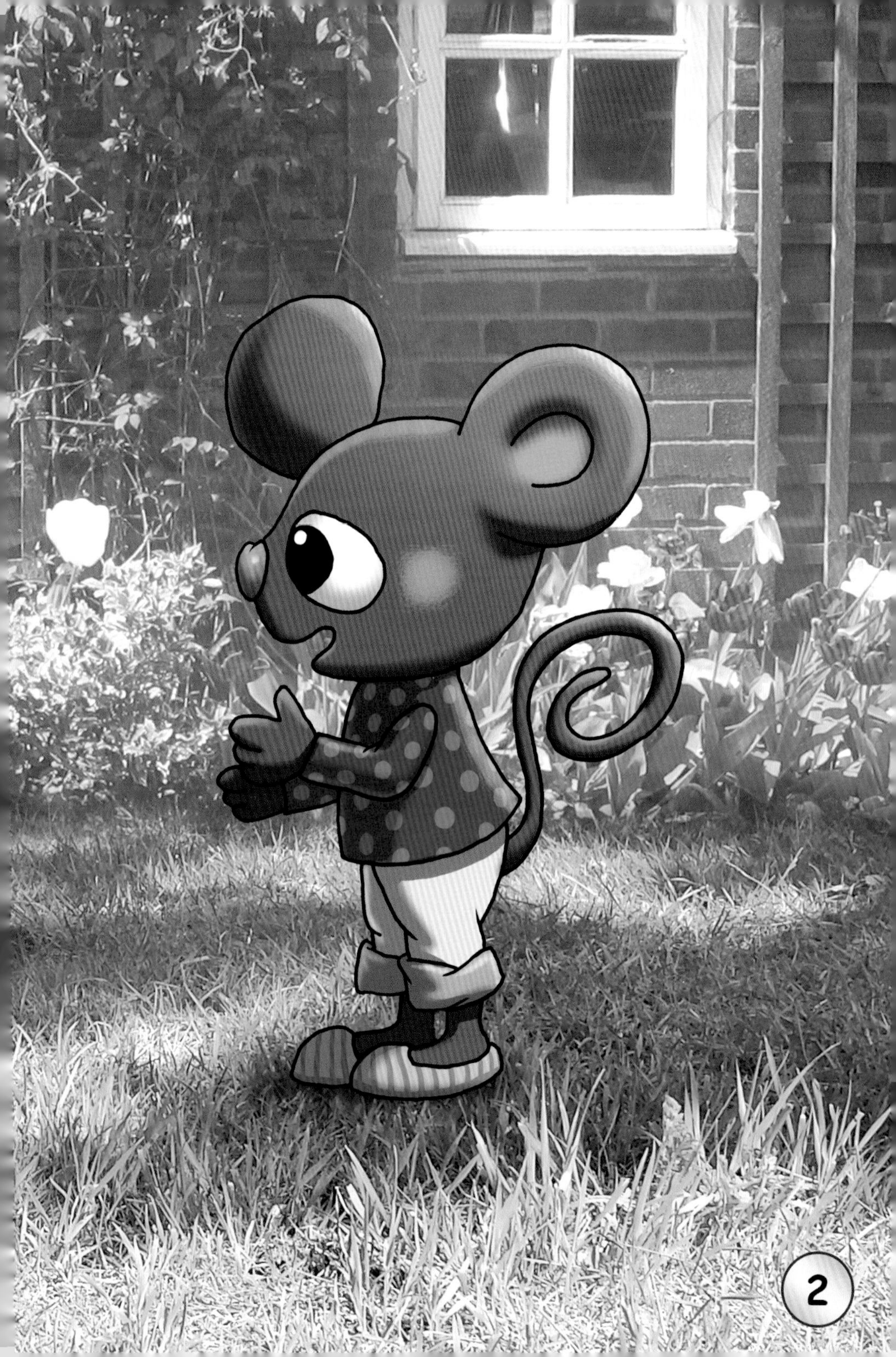

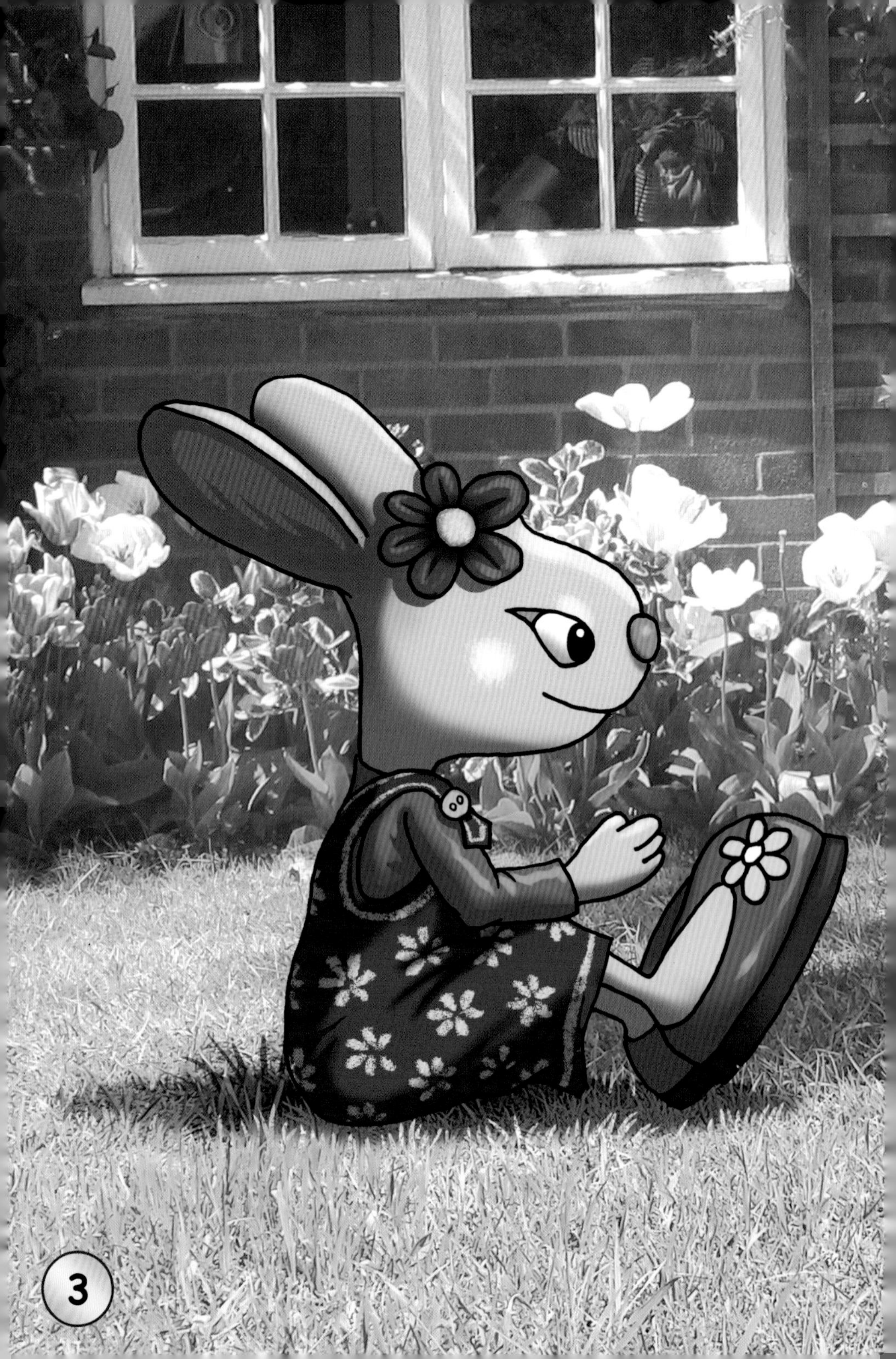

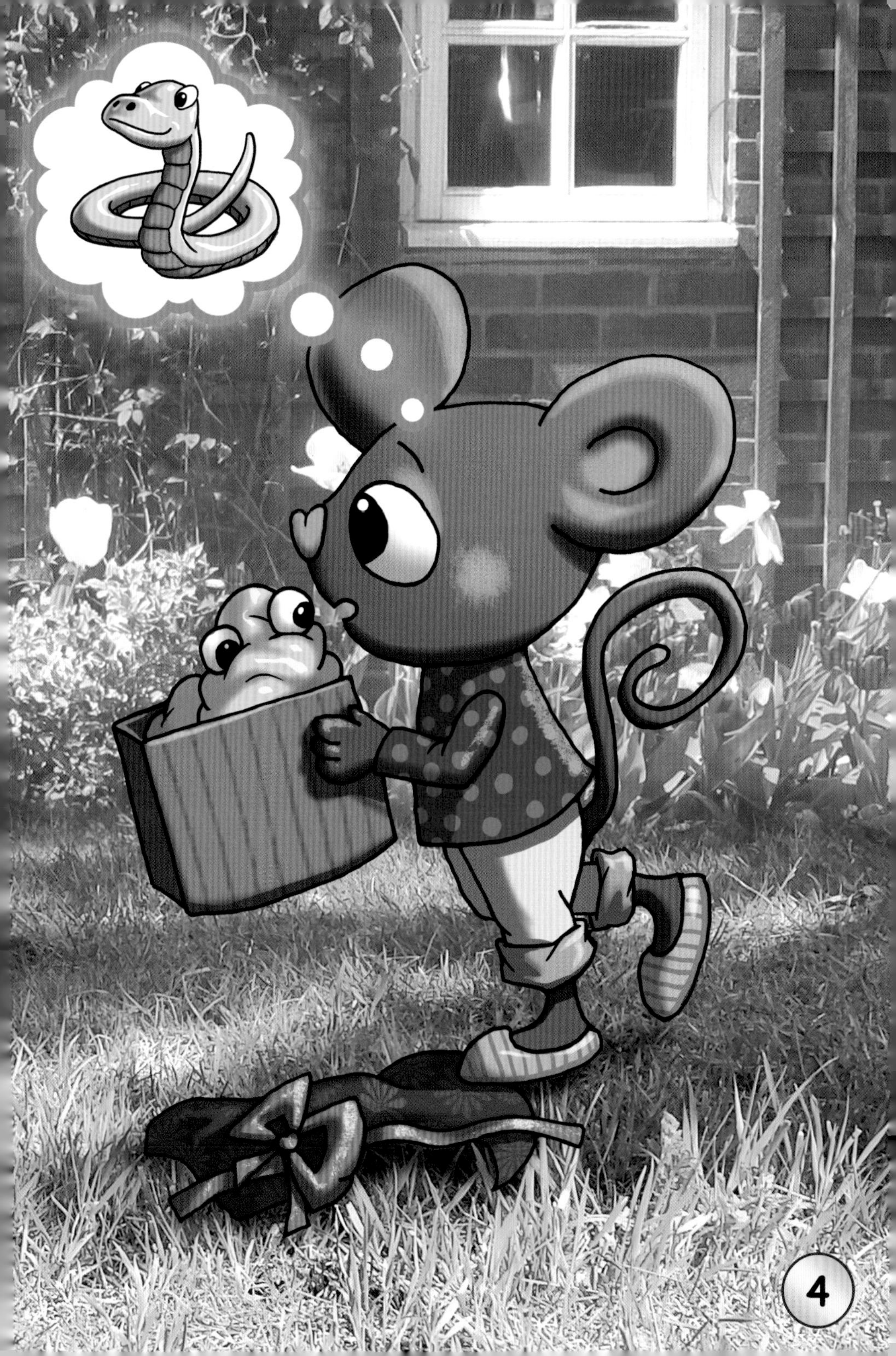

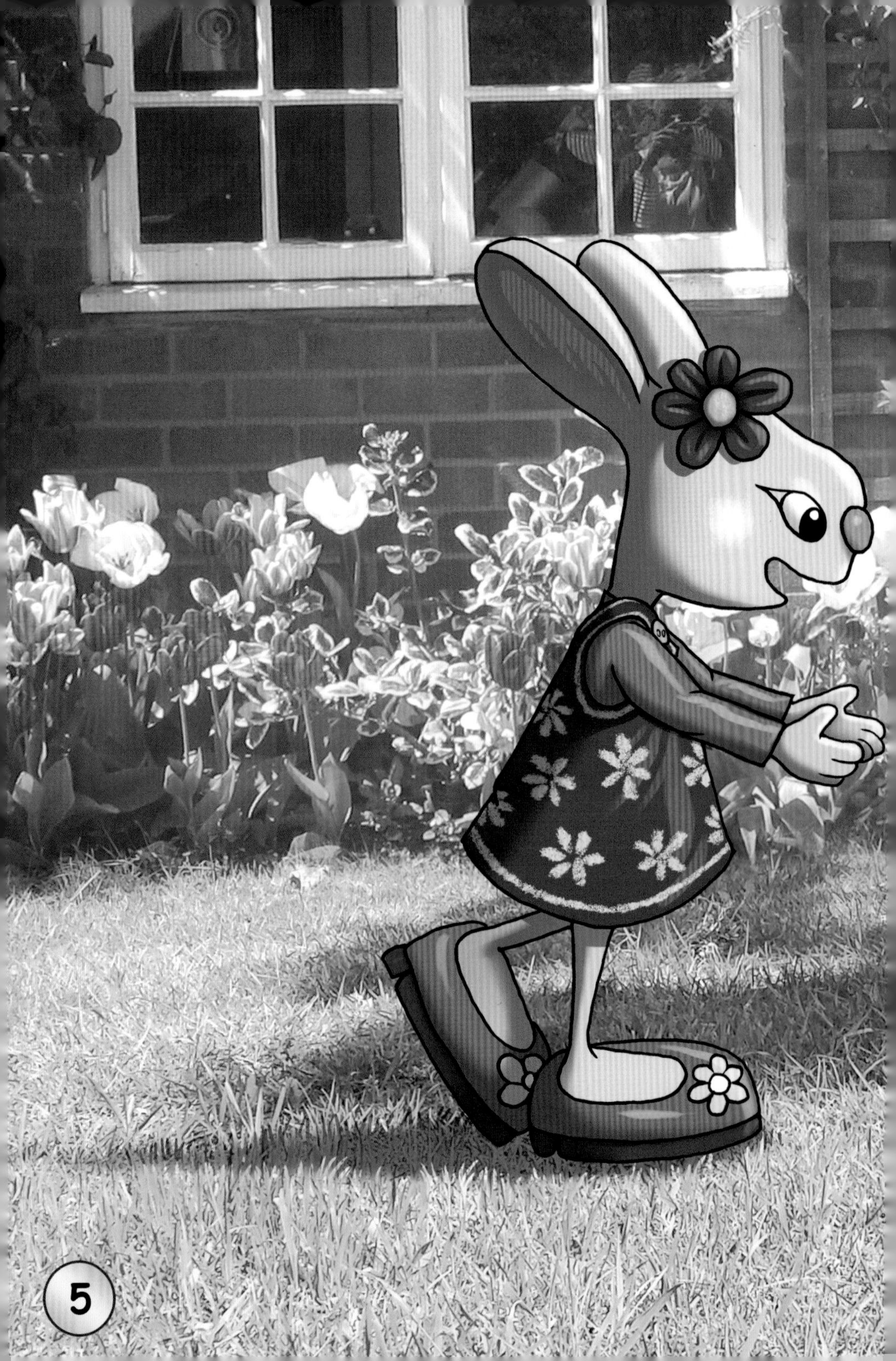

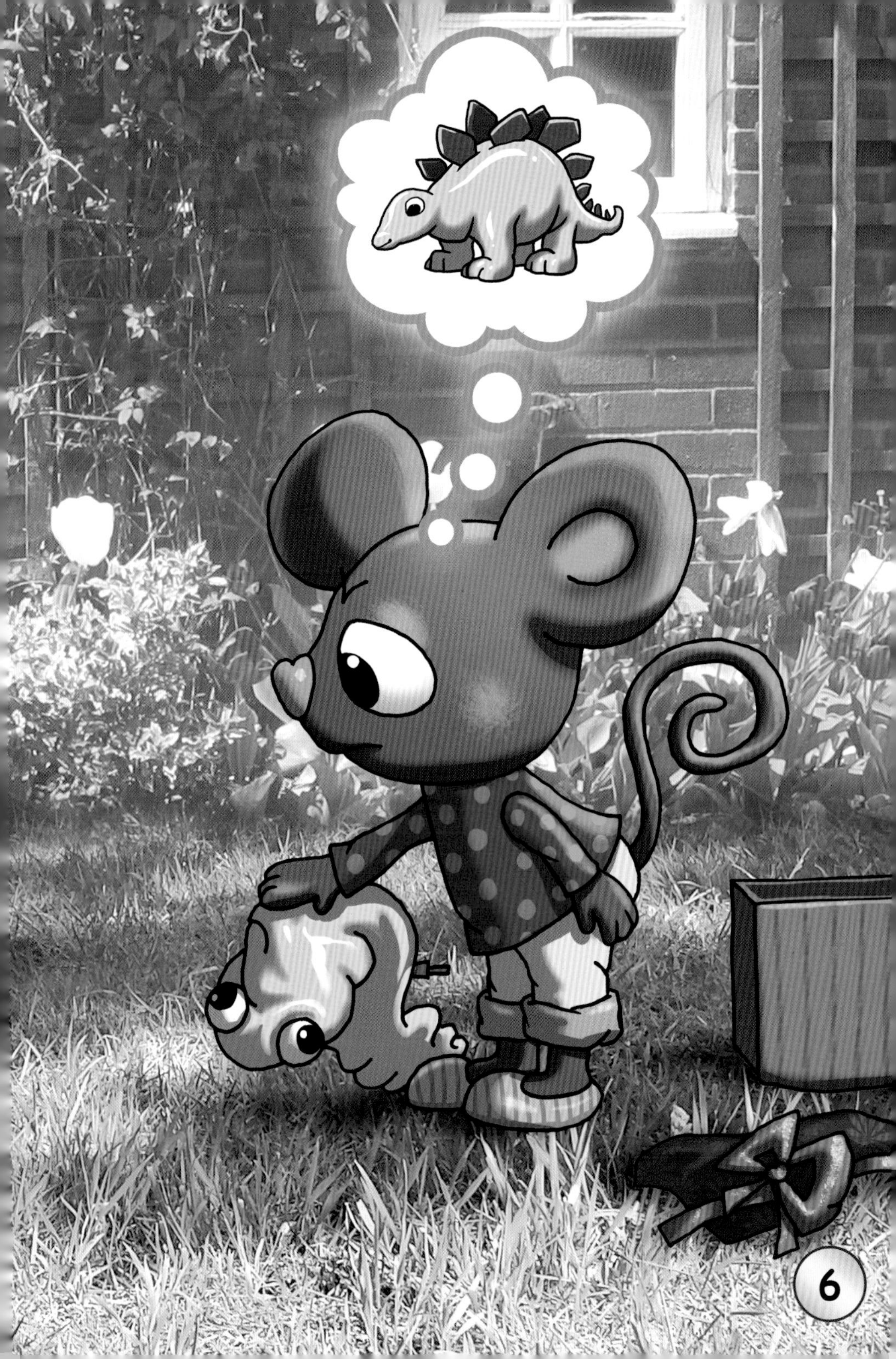

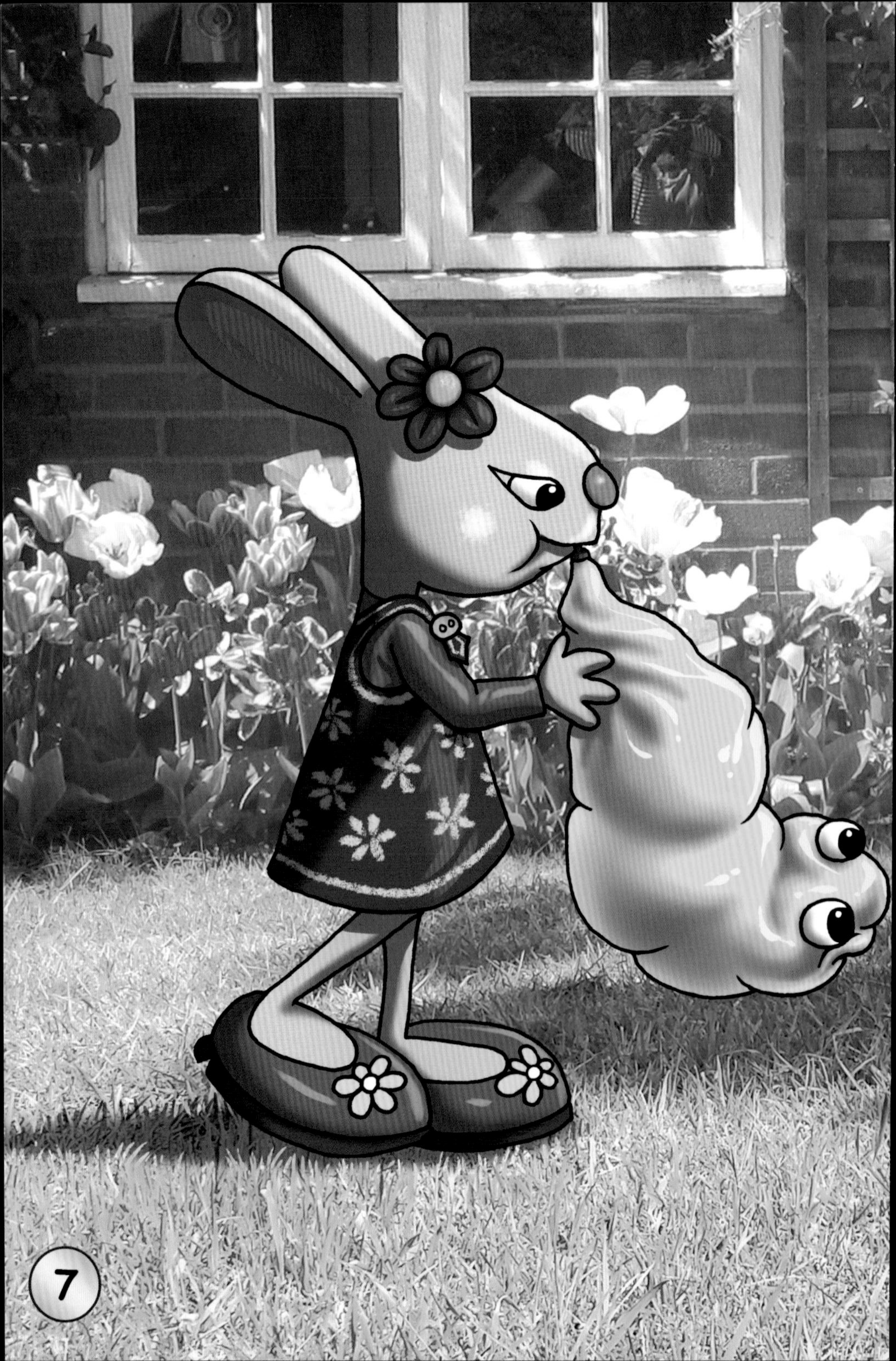

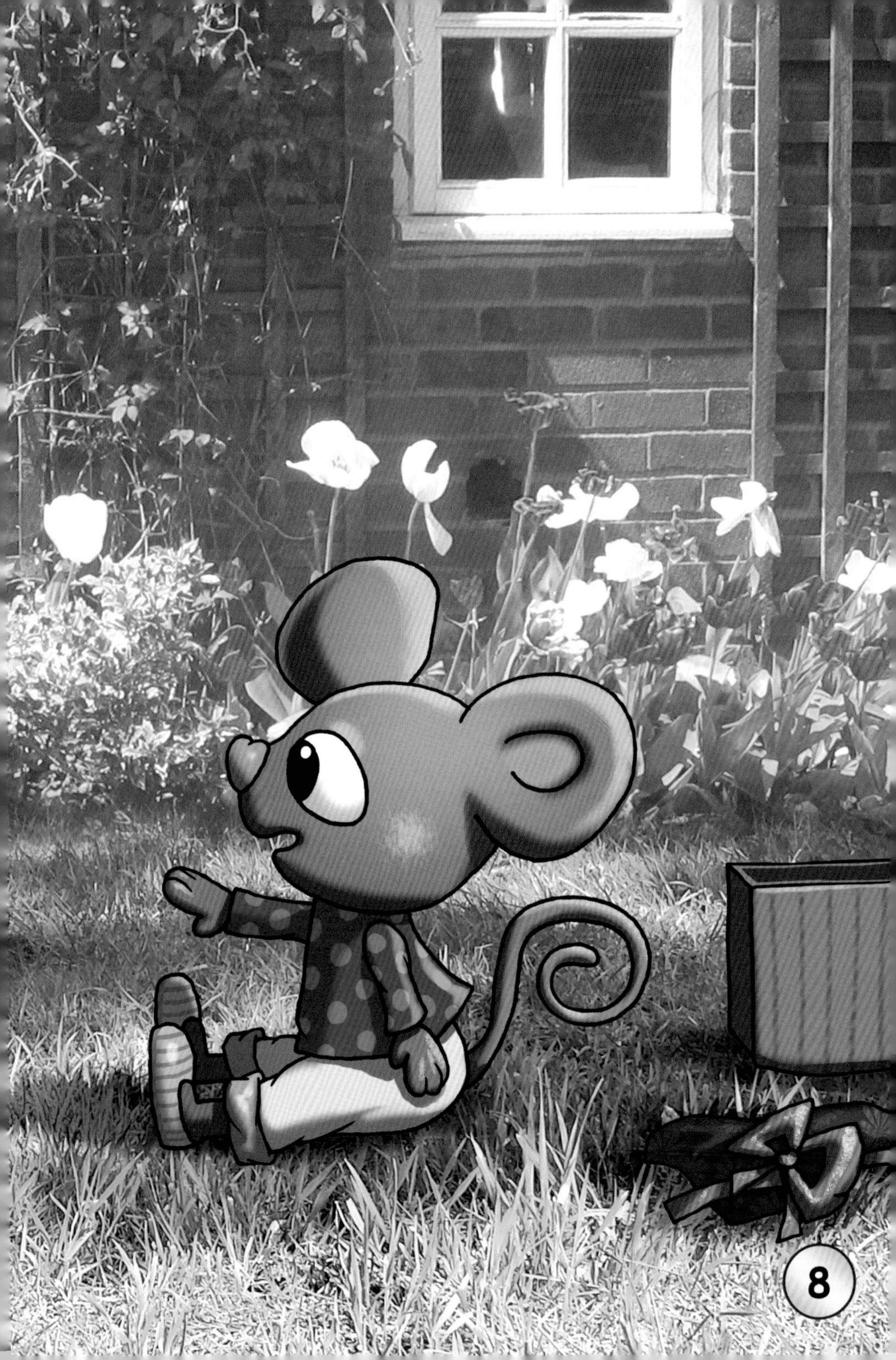

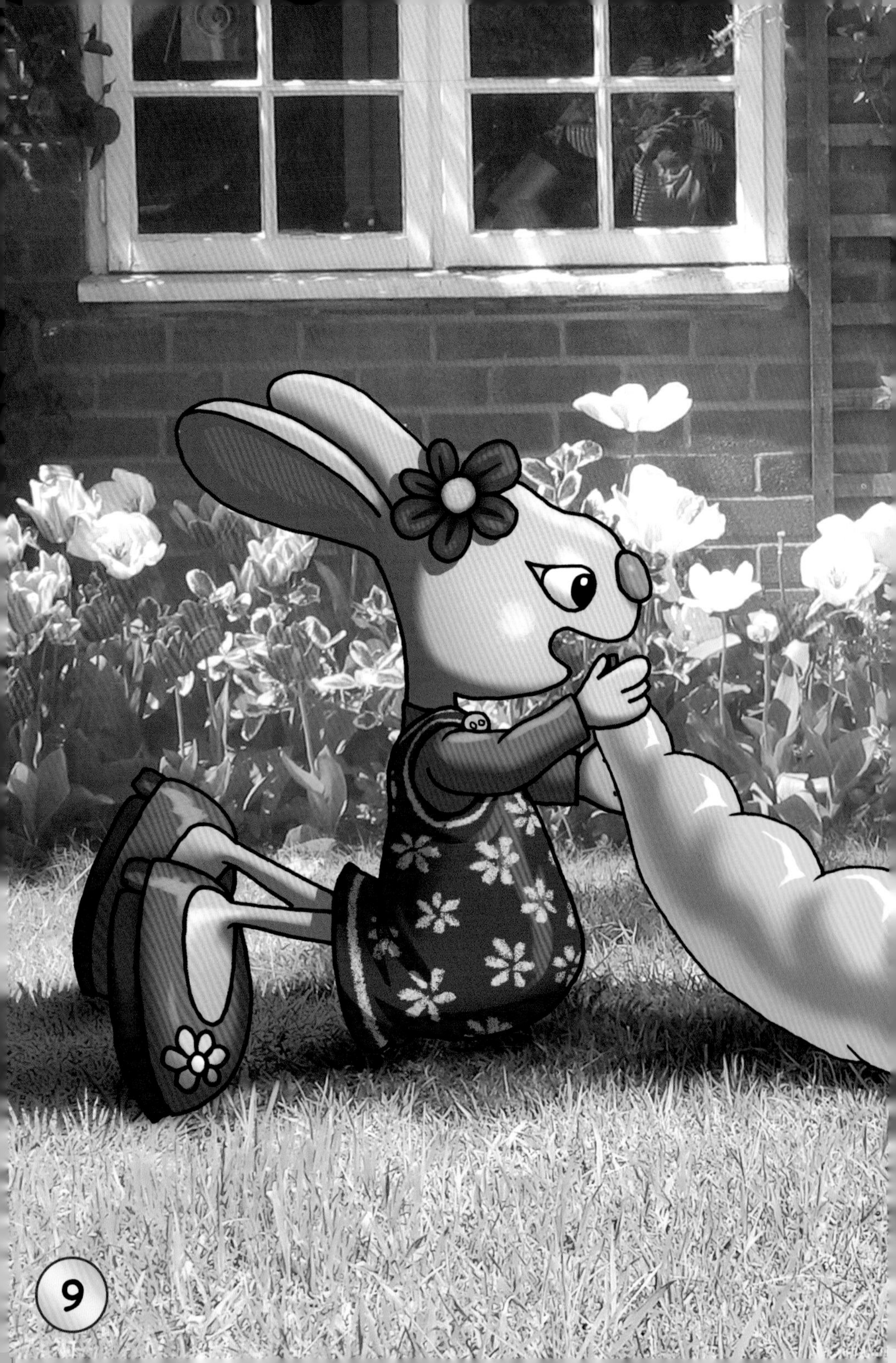

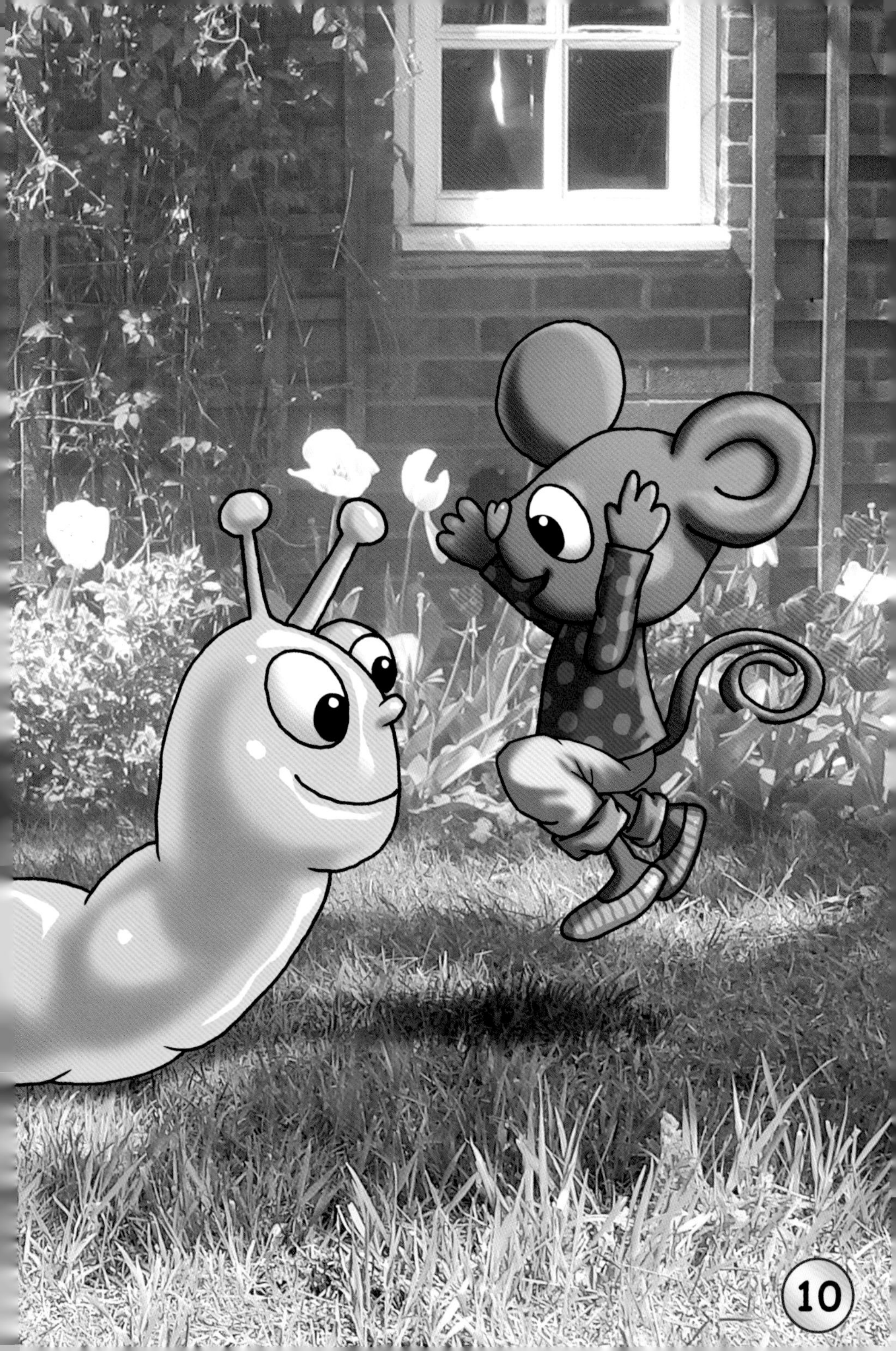

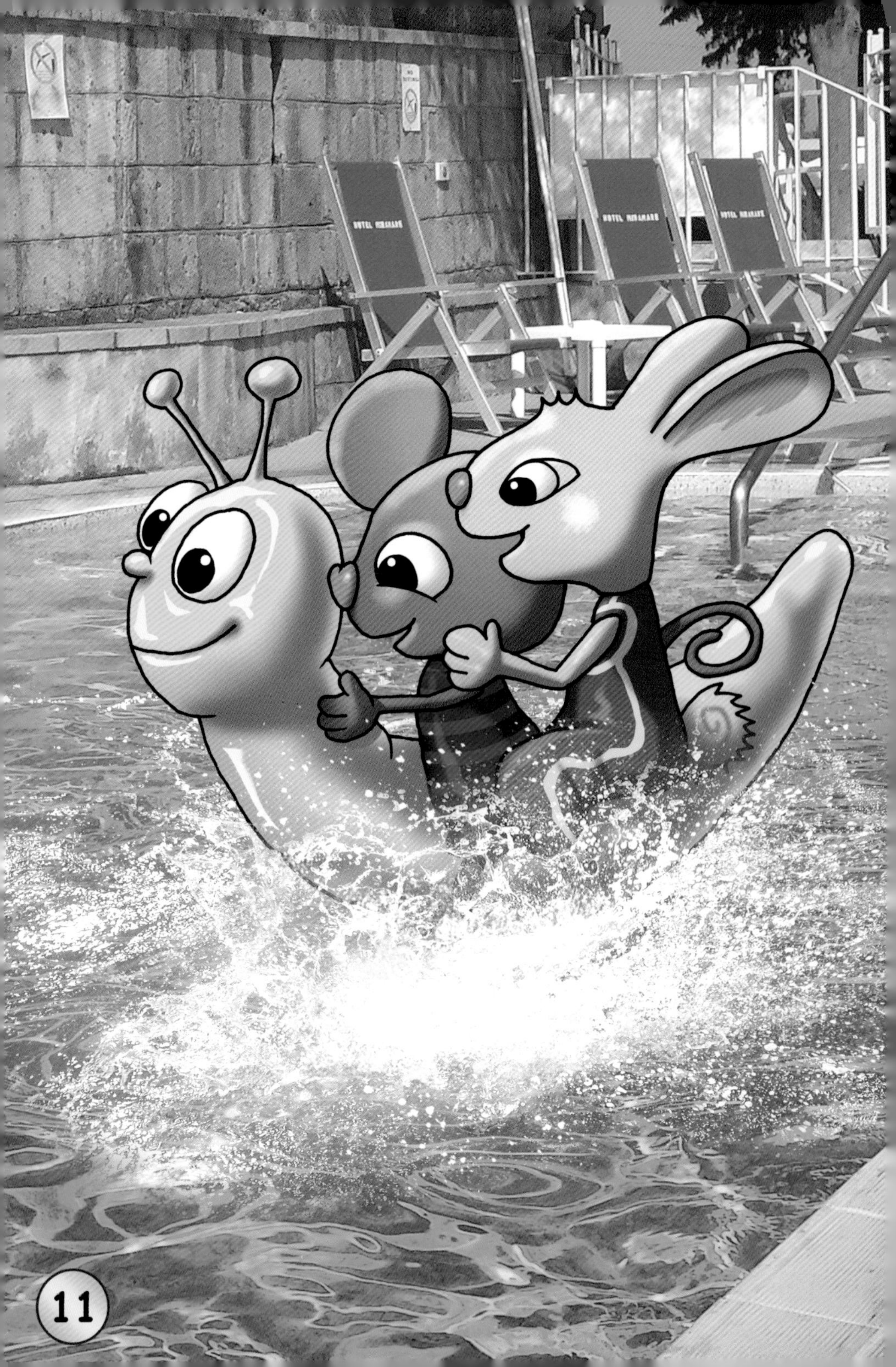